P-Town Diaries

P-Town Diaries

by

Corey Spears

One Spirit Press
Portland, Orgon

©Copyrighted 2006-2011 by Corey Spears

All rights reserved
Printed in the USA

ISBN 978-1-893075-18-4
LCCN: 2006938945

Book Design: Spirit Press, LLC
Cover Design: Aaron Yeagle

This book may not be reproduced by electronic or any other means which exist now or may yet be developed, without permission of Spirit Press, except in the case of brief quotations embodied in critical articles and reviews.

One Spirit Press
www.onespiritpress.com
Portland, Oregon

Dedication

I would like to dedicate this work to Matthew Kelleher, Jimmy James, Bubba McNeely, Lady Bunny and Christopher Ciccone who made the summer of 2003 so special. Also, special thanks to Andy Braun for his patience with me whilst putting this book together.

Forward

When I was growing up in the Deep South, my grandmother was fond of telling me "life was not a bed of roses." Over the years, I began to take that age-old sentiment to heart as I came to realize that her sage advice could not have been more prescient. With time I came to understand the verity of my grandmother's message as I began to develop the tools necessary to take in the fact that life was not only about the good, but also about the bad and everything in between and that every hurdle I faced in life presented an opportunity for me to become stronger than I had ever thought previously possible.

And as I grew emotionally with each challenge that life presented to me, I came to comprehend the unifying power of art and expression to translate universal experiences. For me, art became about conveying the raw, palpable emotions that define the human experience… the real…the honest…the painful…the joyous…the transcendent moments…that humanize us all in spite of the superficial world surrounding us that can so easily defines us should we allow it to.

Put more simply, there is perhaps no better way to describe art than to say that, in its purest form, real art touches the soul and in the process captures the very essence of a moment in time and all of the complexities those special moments bring with them. And this is the very reason that I consider Corey Spears' "P-Town Diaries" both a resounding success and a triumph, not only because of the man behind the words but also because of the unique ability of the words spawned by the man to transport the readers of those words to a unique and provocative space in time.

Love, loss, grief and pain are emotions that every human being will experience in a lifetime if they are open to them. In "P-Town Diaries" Corey Spears takes readers on a summer long journey through those emotions in a brilliantly touching way that without artifice or pretense shows the vulnerability of a man willing and able to brave the hurdles of love despite an inner sensibility which fights all notions of romance or fairy tales. Corey's poetry enraptures because it epitomizes the conundrum that comes with a love affair that shows itself just when it is least expected. This poetry is about the age old tales that have spawned love anthems like Deborah Cox's "Nobody's Supposed to Be Here" and Whitney Houston's "Saving All My Love For You" as well as the very heart of what we now call the romantic comedy.

To be fair, I must say that I feel a part of the poetry contained in "P-Town Diaries" because I experienced so many of the moments chronicled in this collection of poems with Corey as they happened. As he wrote the poetry contained in this collection, I spoke with Corey by phone almost daily and rode the twisting, turning rollercoaster of emotions with him. At the time, I had no idea that all those conversations would yield such a remarkably unblemished account of his emotions, but now that I've read them it seems only natural that those experiences should have led to such a result.

The extraordinary thing about Corey Spears as both an artist and as a person is that he holds nothing back. He is genuinely what he presents. He is not a chameleon because he never changes his colors. He is not a magician because his charm and appeal has nothing to do with trickery. He is quite simply who he is…unashamed, unafraid and unaffected and his poetry says as much.

When he barreled into my life several years ago Corey charmed me with his down-home persona, his sincerity and his compassion. In a city like Los Angeles, he was a proverbial "breath of fresh air". So it comes as no surprise that his poetry subscribes not to tradition but to heartfelt creative expression. "P-Town Diaries" is a stringing together of life experience and genuine emotion, told by a man…a real man… who has loved, lost and dared to love again.

Through his body of work and his life, Corey Spears has demonstrated that life is about living and surviving and not merely just about getting through and he has never reflected that experience in any other medium better than he has in "P-Town Diaries". I dare you to read this collection and not see yourself and the power of human interaction within it, because like the writer of these passionate words, this is a collection that is honest almost to a fault, real to the point of true vulnerability and as refreshingly sincerely as an "I love you" between lifelong lovers.

Duane Wells
Features Writer, GayWired.Com &
Editor-In-Chief, ListenDarling.Com (July, 2006)

P-Town Diaries

Just a Moment

docks and bays and hotel rooms
feeling my head and chaining my heart
I want to feel it all again
like then.
the smells and the mood, the candles and your touch
your skin and how you kissed my neck
I want to feel this in my hands.
the rush and twist of my heart
ah to know once more how we lay together in the sand
moonlight shining all around us
I feel all of these now
for just a moment.

untitled 6/04

tight at the center.
in your gut.
pulled tight.
then twisting with great force.
removing your air
eventually you lose consciousness
yet you do not care
the apathy startles you.
you are contorted into odd figures
you do not resemble yourself
you do not know yourself
lower still and yet again, apathy covers you.
you put your hands to the sky and want
for hope or faith
they are nowhere to be found.
there is light
dull and exhausted, you want for sleep
it haunts you with unfortunates and wincing
you want to leave.
yet you do not care.

Both of Us

moving on and making way is tiresome
my heart is strong, my heart is weary.
my soul sings truth for a few months
then gives out.
there is no endless supply of energy to these places:
the heart. the soul. the mind
we are tired and want to be left alone
we wanted the most
and we traveled to get there while listening
to our favorite songs
and when we got there
the love had changed.
and now messages in the night,
and unsure hearts,
cross paths of the love once made.

Heartbreak

we ran to the sea
and there it was, our place
the location of all that grew with such spontaneity
it immediately led us elsewhere
we ran into the black forest
and there it was just as I suspected.
impossibility was washing my ideals away
we ran into your heart
it was warm and benevolent and could easily be my home
yet there was no space for me there.
we ran inside my head
it was dazzling and adventurous
but unpredictable and unsettling for you
so now in minor keys, our song plays
with you, one heart and an entire land mass between us.
I stare out at the sea and watch for a change of tides.

Encore

looking at my wrist I see no time for this.
I warn, do not sneak up on me with your loaded hands.
I have seen this look in the eyes of others before
now I am running
yet your speed paces my every motion
chases me down.
I have nothing in my power to withstand
so I relent.
again.

untitled 7/04

I know words, like swords,
can either be used for pain or protection
think of this when I am there
do I cut or shield?
do I project or provoke?
now I sit in purple clouds and know not my next move
(is anyone counting on it anyway?)
I hear harps and the occasional angel.
I know the symphony and occasionally the orchestra
I do not know however, what exactly takes place
in love or how beauty changes so quickly.
yet I write of passion, and romances, and candlelit showers
and making love on the beach
but does this save me from illegitimacy?

Lately

fingertips on his skin.
cool air on my legs.
wishing for summer.
waiting for love.
too much sun and not enough color.
the harsh mix of this place has taken its toll.
now I wait for beauty or inspiration to offer me solace.
the only change of color takes place in my mind.
softly, so softly these days pass, and their impact on time
is a death blow to what could be a future.
I can remember when it all had such push
and dreaming was living
yet now I walk in gardens of gray.
breathing in all that overwhelms my capacity.
I have not the fortitude nor the key.

untitled 8/04

the truth is in me
I am the truth
these words are ready for their release into air
they look good against a blue background; the sky
truth abides in me and I abide in truth
I want to know the truth of the clouds
and the sky as they faithfully stay with us.
to abide in the truth of the moon as it changes
and controls my lovelife.
ultimately the sea is my truth
and I must abide in the sea with its every wave
that crashes onto the beach.

Go Ahead

there aren't enough stupid pills to take
and this pen smears across the page
every inch of its tracks
has your image and attitude
and even your smile
it's happy throughout, so do not twist these words
we do not frown upon this, but
please let my heart go for it can do much more when it is free
not bound
bound by kisses. and laughter
and of course your scent and your thighs and that curve of your
cheek.
trying to sleep and not have these sweet attributes crowd me
is simply awful
the adulation that has filled my pages, warmed my soul
and redefined serenity is all yours.

untitled 3 / 04

you will find it hard to sleep tonight
without my face to roll into
my feet that have secret meetings with your own
our mutual need for aid in sleeping certainly makes it difficult.
my friend, my lover here we are stretched out a bit
with a chorus directing me to all different directions
but I ultimately can carry it all without them
my voice is rich and has texture
so there will be a listener for some of the messages
moreover, I mean I will be here for that listener and he knows that
but is he here with me?

Goodnight to You

goodnight to you
your precious heart slows
I am here you are not
I stroke your head
and watch your peace
the touch taking you deeper
to that space where
I am here and
you are too
I kiss your mouth
an exhale from you
is as light as a whisper
to my ear
that says indeed it was love.
I agree and say
goodnight

The Sea Watches Over Me

I am glad the sea watches over me
while I sleep
I have tried to free you from this equation
me + love + my heart +
you are the missing increment
I feel ready to set sail and again
be at sea with my livings
I look back to see you there and my voyage is
rescheduled.
I am beached.
mercy to me and mine as we await
our inevitable journey.
for now I sleep and the sea watches over me

Why I Am Pulled Out

grabbing my heart and twisting tighter
though I look at your picture and smile
I think about a question and the answer
is an emphatic yes
every inch complements the next.
smooth to the touch and textured all the same
(unconditionally it is happening)
your body arranged by the gods surely
arms that ripple with strength
to kiss this stomach is blissful
your willing skin pulls me closer
to the perfect bend
that fills every trench that accepts graciously
stripped of all esthetics the realness
of this beauty is palpable.
the skin is flawless and unparalleled
removing my ability to form rational thought
how can I give you all my love if I am
turned upside down
do not look at me without letting me know,
so I can prepare my heart.
turn me into a child
take away my wings
yet I still fly.
all of this because of the joy of knowing you

The Luckiest Time Continues To Repeat

I came in from the rain that pours with
indefinite weight since you said no more
here I am in the only place I can see you now
none the less, we are out of the rain
smiling, you greet me
angelic
now you are selling food from a vending station
your eyes as green as ever
your shirt is white
you ask how much I liked the plethora
of gifts I received from your parents
for Christmas
I say that I gave half of them back
my heart filling with every word
each sentence a lifetime of healing
you ask if you can get me anything
I decline
I am just not hungry

The luckiest time continues to repeat II

If you were to wake next to me you'd
find me waking with a smile
but the amount of breaths that have passed through me since then
are innumerable - much to my chagrin.
All I have are parasympathetic expressions that lead me to a
beach with miles of sand like talc
I am on your shirtless back
speaking freely into your ear
38 miles and mouths pressed together
and I still taste you on my breath now
The sea is on both sides of us
one side is silent, while the other is spectacular and
symphonic.
Each ripple of your musculature matches the sand -
as if both could only be perfectly arranged by nature itself
and though envy pours out of me in the form of "her" and "him"
I walk away with you and
you hold my hand.

The luckiest time continues to repeat III

could these be simultaneously occurring?
you come to me in dreams
more beautiful than ever
all the confusion still intact
leading me through neighborhoods you have long since moved from
I walk under half built structures and between frames with spider webs covering them
a labyrinth of what I have dreamt and what I am now really dreaming.
I touch you and it is like my hands never left
the smell, the hair on your legs tickling me
your smooth stomach with perspiration dripping, seducing
almost daring me to try and chase
In this space below consciousness we meet
I awake again and know you were there too.
I feel spider bites from earlier.
My ears ring from that train that runs in front of
your new house.
all day I am nervous and bite off all of my nails.
But now I am ready-
ready to meet you again tonight.

Break away

please show me
I impress upon you
even the strongest among us do break
is it not hard enough to make each day pass?
standing there like an angel
I will open every door and touch your hand
loyalty; watching the world handed to you
I am yours
like roots for trees.
grow, reach, continue
greetings from treasured hosts
I step back; there for you.
precious, the implacable freshness of honey colored skin
controls like seasons.
there he is now and nothing is any good
crying and paying for sins.
drenched in sorrow. please come out
please show me
wipe away tears with my love of beauty
it is safe now
you will not be torn apart or neglected
someone to hold you with arms that praise the touch of your skin
careful, kind, when you need someone to pull you through
you are free now

The First Time / Somerset

lit only by candlelight
we are wet and steamy
in this surprise within a gift
water trickles down your rippling body
and splashes in between my toes
we are slick with soap and climb into
each other so quickly.
your face opens my usually locked walls
and your words can speak of no one else
no other time no other place, but of me and my heart
possessed by a power we have no resistance to
we are forced into a mystical love affair with a rhythm of its own
we are awake and smiling
we both feel we just made love
and it turns out we did.

Before Bed

cool wind on my resting body
encompassed in white and pale blue
my short hair massages the pillow with sounds
looking at my hands I see thirty years of living, loss and love
every day leaving their mark.
my past ventures are again knocking on the door
with their friend opportunity.
I lift my legs to feel sweet cold linen
gently caressing.
I hear the knocks and will reply
but first I must breathe and enjoy the place between breaths
where I make a life

Glow

I heard you
now that you have little messengers
you need not utter a sound
a direct line from heart to soul
you lit this flame
still burning
still lighting
it glows even in your absence
your thoughts feed this flame
whether or not they are spoken makes no difference
they were pushed out into space
the space that has an orbit around two hearts
they feel every pulse as if they were one
why say anything?
just as it becomes a thought it is instantly felt in me.
all of me, and every truth that is me
is now your truth and is now all of you.

from my lips

I hope the kindness in my heart can redeem
all the words that have escaped from my lips
the twists and turns of a road wound around
a multitude of wounded days and unrest.
the thickest light has touched me
and now I know that from my lips
have escaped my chance.

Letter to a lover

you know I love you
and I pull as much of you
to my heart that waits.
I could never be cold.
The depths hold me from seeking another.
My own seeks yours.
Yet you are a shadowy reminder of what I used to see-
your smile has changed and so have the thoughts behind your eyes.
The blueness becoming cold.
I cannot keep score at this
out of sight could mean out of mind.
(perhaps that is the only place you ever were)
my life should never make you wander
Is there a piece of you inside of me?
am I losing you?

Next to me

I will sleep so deep and wish that you were here, but for now you are...
next to me
peacefully dreaming, holding me.
feeling soft skin against you with firm muscle
hardening us both
dive into my mouth with your tongue, seeking, pulling
breathe my air, a sexual gasp; I exhale your breath
sucking in your strawberry flavored tongue.
licking flesh, the scent of us swirls in the air
like perfume..."do you feel that?" I ask and
the response is "ya." No designs for such
things can be drawn up much to your chagrin.
Happening out of nowhere they continue down
to heaving chests and welcoming stomachs, kissing
stroking. Taking me in your hands pulling out
a fantasy while putting in your bed.
I lay atop of you feeling you beneath me
between my legs; sticky and warm; relieved entirely
At times there are no words just long gazes into
pools of blue that keep you soft and cool.
Here, next to me.

Nature's first gift to us/ interlude 1

technology seeps from this mind in the same way
beauty from his skin, completely naturally
a laugh that incites laughter to follow
tendrils of gold drape cheekbones that are perfectly
structured around red-wine lips with plumpness that dares me
to kiss them.
I did!
under a full moon
exchanges of comparable existences
sand as our chair
no need for a blanket
we wrap around each other for warmth
hearts beating together
lips pressed
hands holding
the glow of the moon brightens and we dance away
telling the ocean good night
it crashes back
we drive and park
Unstoppable, your hands, my speedo
my face, your thighs
mounting our beginnings.

re introduce

Had I never loved that way
I probably would not be like this nor
would I hurt so bad
everybody thinks I have gone mad
I want to move yet there is no escape.
If I'd never seen your face I would never
be this way.
You should see how people look at me.
Even when I have these rendezvous you are there.
Sometimes I see you standing in front of me.
there is so much power in your gaze and yet when it fixes on me
I feel depleted and full at the same time.

The Last Kiss

twas not the man nor the time.
those places and what they bring.
those emotions and the surge of creation.
those lips and the sweetness they push.
allow it to open and happen and not be
weighed down with why the last kiss taken and was numbing
but open to the experience of and the love of and the sheer beauty of
the last kiss.
xx.

untitled 3 / 04

It comes out and of course
I listen
probably from you
maybe from me.
almost like drugs
the high that beats on.
slicked back hair
and tanned skin
beautiful as always.
the nicknames stick and apply
your address rules this peace
rules, restrictions and beliefs never befit me
they never have
but you and your fleet
take me out to sea and
pump out what you need
and have me
like fields have grass
fish have water
you have me.

nothing comes close

I have searched to find the touch
I have tried to kiss the lips
I have opened myself to the love
opened for the connection
if even for a night.
but you see, nothing comes close
I want to hold those hands and I see them in mine now.
I want to feel those legs against mine in embrace.
I know their warmth.
I want that nervous movement and assured gaze in my eyes
and I find again
nothing comes close.
Wishing on every star - even the ones that fall from the sky
Looking to the sun especially those setting in pink clouds
Praying to all the gods trying the ones I never knew, even still, nothing,
nothing comes close.

untitled 11 / 05

I look for the oceans of serenity that soothe me when
I am bleeding - almost literally, from inside.
I immediately think of you and hope that the thoughts will somehow
make what I have done
less detrimental.
It almost works.

Strange Fruit

Bitter and sweet this tongue that
has tasted you and those like you.
Nothing unfamiliar about the portion
you presume to be special.
yet the harvest that has fed plenty,
barely quenches the slight and almost deniable thirst I have.
It is blatant to me that these gifts that fall ripened off
the vine are not for me to taste.
Not without
leaving my mouth barely quenched
and my heart hard and full of contempt for the tree that produces
such strange fruit.

you are not the only one

I have the other ones that come
they find me in my space and dance with my needs.
He dances with my choice, not my fate.
he visits not to fill in,
I am already full.
But to open me is impossible at this juncture as IT prefers to be with ITself.
Teasing me - pleasing them
they come here and I let them ... all of them ... but the winds are blowing me to my sea.
I am alone at sea...and it is beautiful.

it is time

more than a passing glance
more than a smile
more than a touch
more than words
more than passion
more than silent breaths
more than a kiss
more than affection
more than whispers in my ear
more than love
more than possible
more than ever.

amazing

I wanted to believe in you
maybe even your details.
Isn't that where you are supposed to be?
I guess you are in disguise.
But never revealing yourself.
There is no savior
Nor any messiah.
You have left.
I am not open to your suggestions.
My reflection has walked away
Your love is not going to set me free.
Time will not tell.
Mass hysteria has yielded blindness to all who are available
to your insatiable needs.
I think Your absence is amazing.

sacred

If held in your heart
is it not sacred?
If held in your palms
is it not valuable?
Why these things would change baffles even the intelligentsia.
If your air, then why not you?
If my heart, then why not me?
It does this and I flow from there
to this pen and keep moving to find
What is sacred?
What is valuable?
What is in my heart?

the first new love poem I can write

you can not see a beginning
it was already in motion
perhaps there is that love
the one that took no time to find
it came to you
from nowhere
from paradise
its apparently still there
and do I wait?
my heart is activated
that one love is alive
it beats for you in me
What a gift to feel inside
the one that is in you with simultaneous movement
I am sensitive to it and its purity
That one love that was opened up and
resides in you and waits for me.
If you touch my hand and grasp all
that was waiting will pass into your
heart and again respond
as it did before.

tidal changes

I need not write in red
The words are clear in the direction
will growth ever supersede the heart?
touched by your show of honesty
Done so without breach of any contract
Our time need not be now.
Our time is.
When I am where you are,
in that moment, at that hour,
that ocean I've swum before will
settle into shores that long
for this change of tides.
The tides....they are in motion.

sea me again

my only ocean and its tides
they crash and I hear you
I swim and you are all around me...cold...and wet
sometimes on my feet
sometimes in my hair
The sun is bright and I squint and I can see you.
I swallow sea water and taste you.
All that is you is in the oceans...all oceans
every truth that is you
is told to me
in each break of the waves

I see the next falling star

The light was blue and low
dazed but certainly clear and familiar
did I dream that?
did you mean that?
there was no hesitation on my lips
nor your tongue
melting together and flowing effortlessly
it is so deep
deeper than any amount of control
not quite as maddening to me now
I can look now into those eyes without worry
even stares will not flinch
I felt drawn to your mouth
perhaps to touch your lips or take the kiss which
occurs with all the predictability of
a falling star.

dance to leaving

you dance together
slowly
you both know
I am watching
swaying hips
stomachs tightening, legs locking
unusual groove complements unusual coupling
I whisper in his ear softly
he smells so nice
that area on his neck by his ear and his hairline
I want to kiss it.
you still dance
his back to me.
when he turns,
I will still be here.
watching and waiting.

bitter

I do not want to fuck
I want to disregard
schedule that in
I do not want to reveal
I cannot listen to my ego
I want a chain of guardians
My peace is there
I want you to reveal
and listen and want
I haven't much time
I do not know for sure
I never liked lying
I always do
I cannot chase anything
I want it in my path
to be devoured or delighted in
or despised or indifferent to.
silent and ignored
loud and ignored
justly ignored
they call and I don't care.
they don't care.
sarcastic cycle.
I feel the shift.

on this epicycle

I can't tell if it's ending or opening up even more
so many fantastic turns
rare consistencies keep rearing their heads
secrets reveal themselves and nobody flinches
brilliant and stupid all in the same
faster
slower
sudden and prolonged
more breath to change
more breath to find things the same
cyclical and contradictory
decorated and raw
Is there grace?
I lap it up with a seemingly unquenchable thirst.

like paradise

cradle me
warm and perfect
I like your blue push
with a little white
My red is a generous mix in this virtual color chart
peace to my heart
slow to my head
winds carry the scents of love being formed all around
guava has my lips my sticky and sweet
unexpected formula
golden tan for winter minds
sun bleached hair for winter eyes
I smell miles and miles of desolate beach
and it is so fresh.
like paradise.

powerful

gentle words that flow from trembling lips
ground down like sand to fine powder
my wishes to keep still ignored by my
desire to move forward
make my flesh irrelevant
make my soul rise and take charge.
mate of the soul? or instigator of creation-
either way, down on my knees, I will
beg for my senses to return, my heart to beat
realistically, and for you to touch me
again and move me to tears.

no net

I could not predict a more sacred love
one that takes all that dared to be called love,
and reminds it that this new one will permeate with
a force that nothing should be compared to.
now
then
tomorrow
the magic you've cast makes no delineation in time.
a place with nothing flat
everything rich, vibrant, flowing
Here we go from shore to shore
love navigates what little control we've given without grudge.
how smooth, how perfect
No one will find us. Nothing but light and
the smell of sea air is left behind.
Breathing life into all we touch.
what was wilted is now in bloom.
like heaven.
like the sea.
Fall as if heaven and the ocean are your net.
They are.

Endlessly

Here's where it goes when inside must come out
I put it here because inside is too small
Inside is making room
Its been twisted into something inexplicable.
Trying to make sense of so much beauty and adrenaline and desire
and longing.
When did you switch me?
Your lucky match?
your unfortunate flame?
Creases of strength and sweetness
make me know how much I am.
Lick your lips, do your thing
the one that keeps all others at bay.
Not that I can ensure my love, but if you keep crashing into my
shores, the surely my love, all my love
will be yours endlessly.

what color?

Is it the blue that melts pink
into sunsets?
gold mixed into purple
bouncing off green ocean to brilliantly light your face;
shining, cancelling...
How lucky, how accidental.
What color came out?
Red swears away any yellow that dares to come to its show
Burgundy decides you're not worthy and tells everyone.
Blue soaks me and you.
Its too dark to know light...dark, almost black
but nonetheless reflecting spectacular beams
of icy silver and green, hanging on and dancing for us while
we watch and I wonder
what color you see?

p-town shack

standing on these shores
you know we've been here before
but never on this path
on this path are new sights.
great hills of sand with brush that mixes green, straw, and rosehips.
we touch as we walk
we see an empty shack made of wood
with nothing for miles but sand, ocean and stillness.
we find ourselves on the roof
we are naked
Blue sky looks down and assures us that we are alone.
This abandoned shack will play host to
our discovery of private beach bliss
and more so to love.
I pick a flower for you and you give me a rock.
I sing to you while you lay in my lap.
your hair, like golden fleece, tickles my body.
You sleep in the sun making your winter-whitened skin honey colored and bright.
I stroke your head softly and know we are
a part of this perfect moment.

swim

the very core of who you are will forever know this sweet smell
the electricity and charge of that first kiss
rolling tongue that only searches for more
Impressing us. Branding us. Guiding us.
The moment when all existence stopped
because a new world was created
it breathes, it eats, it sees light and touches skin
traces of a past that runs parallel
building tracks for a train that is sure to come
I know this charge runs through you
It passes into your body from head to foot
leaving all flesh between invigorated and completely sated.
The only purity we cannot sully.
It beams, it finds, it dictates.
It heats and cools at the same time
open and precious, this love is brilliant
we dive in.

bring me back

There it is again
ringing and repeating through my brain
it is pitch perfect
the tone so clear
I know this sound so well.
your voice makes this sound
I know where this music comes from
I love this sound
It is spectacular and resonant and
it makes my heart dance.
This music only angels could know.
My eyes need not see for it is in the sound of your voice
that returns me to love.

No heaven can match

are those tears
(or is it raining?)
How can so much flood out of complete drought?
like all the times before, it washes away what was left behind.
I cannot go there again.
It is never too late for redemption (even in the darkness)
When your false heaven closes its doors
I've a place with no boundaries.
The paradise you cannot claim.
running to such peace that you become
blinded by white light
It encompasses and enraptures
this is what your own angel created and
set aside for you
No sermon will teach this nor can
religion provide this
this solace is as soft as water
as strong as earth
and it will stay.
stay for you.

Fear Changes to Love

would you even notice
had I not opened up
was that the plan?
to get inside then leave?
how dare I make such statements
I live in alternate space
when did these things happen?
it is chaos each time you slice me open
to bleed out all the imaginary pain
onto stunned onlookers who knew all along
this death would be
the only escape
escape from the torment that I crave
(apparently in the form of a heart)
then it is gone as quickly as it came
all the poison that spewed out and
burned all surroundings now crystallizes
and shines like celestial beings
with smiles and angels greeting my every step
welcoming me with warmth, light, and love.
Now it must be safe to come out
Out from the dungeon I put myself into
and locked inside with all the hate
is now a palace of safety
in that instant when fear becomes love

The sorrow of these two men

I know the sorrow of these men
one finds his heart sitting in limbo
one whose troubles have yet to touch his light
The light shines on them both
but one will not bask
the sorrow of the man grows
the light of one man stays just as bright as before but he watches in sorrow
as his troubled dark friend leaves him.
(there was always light)
the man in the dark is so far away he no longer sees the light
now the man must search for light in others
he has lost the one who kept him bright and hopeful
the light on the man who wanted was warm, glowing, perfect.
(there was always light there)
he looked for the other but all he saw was darkness
there was no need for him to look anymore - he had all the light his heart could hold
there were better days ahead for the sorrowful man in the dark
though he could not see them.
(there was always light there)
the man in the light continued to light the lives of others.
one night a great storm soared over the man in the dark and he saw flashes
of what he once knew, beautiful light that would lead him to another.
The quiet after the storm settled the heart of the man in darkness.
he slept for 41 nights
he woke the morning of his day of angels.

the man in darkness felt the earth move in his heart for the sight before him.
the other man was the sun and had risen in his eyes.
(there was always light there)
These were the gifts he gave to the man in the dark and his endless night sky
was filled with stars.
the man in darkness was again immersed in light from stars,
the sun and even the moonlight were there at his command
it was the first time someone stayed through his darkness and returned.
they felt their hearts so close and their joy would last til the end of time.
their glasses were again filled with dreams to kiss goodnight.
all the sorrow of these two men had left.
and the night finally meets the morning sun and
there was no more sorrow for the men.
(there will always be light there)

untitled 11 / 03

each day your sweetness comes to me
I become more sure yet more unraveled
making one part as calm as clouds
the other as turbulent as rain
does it deepen or subside?
these motions of a current certain to sweep
us off our feet
like light from a full moon, things are clear
yet somewhat dim and blue
beautiful boy at a playground of his own making
throwing sand and blowing kisses.
whose party can you attend?
staring into your eyes will make me feel green
not with envy, but with growth
fresh, new, almost edible;
hold me again remind me once more
the glow that has captured me
trailed me, and liberated me.
here in front of me, so beautiful,
stunning quick, and wanting to
blend what hearts yearn for with
a rational sensibility
water or earth? they both are
yours to tread.

untitled 4 / 04

I immediately appreciate your features
invite and accept
my heart wants to know that it is appreciated.
I appreciate all beauty, all around, yet I find
it thinks nothing of me
does that not make me beautiful?
one can only recognize in others what is
inherently in themselves.
I see bitterness and it turns my stomach
and I laugh too
does that make me bitter?
I feel embittered by life, yet I see beauty
and feel bitter by the lack of appreciation that
beauty shows to me
but beauty was never known to have manners

Every Five Minutes

it misses me
it calls me and misses me
I miss the drug induced
makeout sessions.
tongues playing, licking and kissing
now I am here with soft sheets
and someone in the living room waiting for me
it is late and they are intoxicated
he is intoxicated on his coast.
I am intoxicated on mine.
I would crawl into bed with him
right now and we would
feel so good
and perhaps feel a piece of that magic again

untitled 4 / 04

to say he is beautiful
is obvious but necessary
skin like ivory; flawless and glowing
and every angle of your face is like sky to be
gazed upon
heart that beats for all in his presence
mother to many but innocent like a child
I watch over you and marvel
in your brilliance
your sorrow is my own
your healing; my breakthrough
how sweet and special to say his name.
more than a vision,
my heart, my friend,
my smile

Careless

time can only tease
what was brought to me in fast fashion
it creeps upon me like some phantom
that wants me to be reminded of loves lost.
does it not have more appropriate actions to take?
then to trap me in moments of bliss
and equal parts despair
youth tempts me and I consider the dare.
that is until the bitterness borne out of what
time so gleefully maligns me with has its
way with my heart
so yes, I will try and be scared and stupid.
but along with the tease of time, comes
memories that create possibilities.
I will surrender to its folly

Untitled 5 / 04

without bounds I move and transform
with limits, I am squashed like sand from waves crashing
it was never my intention to gain or deplete
only to evolve.
not knowing a path, I have moved about
without care and certainly at times grace.
yet at times there are thunderous mistakes
thrown at me and a scolding to follow
I present my child with these gifts
that path and all of its lessons
those lessons and all of their wealth
the wealth and all of its treasures
these treasures that are my life

Smart

I think I am at the new heart
the one that I search
the one that I know
I begin to wonder about
to love and long for.
I smile about this heart.
I am nervous and my face twitches
I feel ugly and raw;
opened by this heart.
I am bleeding
but this heart that supports
those beautiful and weak eyes
this heart which I barely know
yet feel warm when I am next to,
it puts me to sleep at night and perhaps comes to me
in a dream
I think this heart would beat for me
and keep rhythm to my own.

Made Me Love Him

both sides have seen light
this one shines bright and does so alone
looking from the other side which was clouded and confused
I prefer this one, alone
the fairytale and party seem distant
and untrue
my ears ring with silence here.
giving and taking
disillusioned and dizzy.
lying in bed before me, I shake my head in disbelief
looking at both sides,
I realize how little I know

The Only Things I Really Have Are Questions

no chant will bring forth
no kingdom is coming
no prayers are heard
no answers are given
no God above
no gods within
no omnipresence
faith as theory
theory as imagination
this reality as fantasy
where are my guardian angels?
is this life or just a dream?
will I wake up?
can it be controlled?
can I change my destiny?
am I even destined?
will you believe the dream?
can there be no judgments; even of the good?
does there have to be a reason?
Is my apathy really just protection?
have I lost it?
where did it go?
did I have it?
can it be given?
will it kill me?
can it save me?
what do you think?

Slider

is it a season?
something that shifts or turns like tides.
pitiful creature hidden in unspoken fear
substitute paternity driving a future
with no license nor wheels
watching you move like lightning
almost striking, affecting, and then not returning.
those hit only dumbfounded, exhilarated
and burned.
slithering beauty that caresses each temptation
daring them to come to its hole
make no mention of its ruler
its true ruler, that dictates how it must move, and to whom.
drawn by the twisted carcass that was once
the chance of romantic love.
lost causes are but your only chance
when sliding under opportunity
rather than embracing it.

Sleep With You

Cool curves of a blue silhouetted body
sweat from heat that radiates even uncovered
sweet breath drawing me in and out
you pull me close when you realize my distance
I back into you
is this where it spawns from?
this rush of light through my darkened eyes.
pulsating heart against warming flesh
I roll over
now you face me
my hand on your thigh
Then in between your legs to rest securely in your heat
Your exhale is my inhale
Cradled, caressed, trusted.

Now I Am Yours

there you are
you take all of me inside all of you
pressing heart to heart
exchanging truths
don't tell
bigger than we know, it rules us
when we are not looking
and when we do, we relent.
so hard, yet with no hesitation
we walk to an uncertain destiny
that assures me when your eyes whisper to me
they say so quietly "here I am"
then I am yours.

To Start Anew

gather it all now
move without hesitation
not giving up
tears will bear witness to things given to you
I pray for comfort
the strength of many will carry any burden
beloved, enslaved, wise, giving
how you try to shine
so gracefully
your light so visible
so quiet
your first shooting star
the clouds across the moon
the miracle that made love inevitable
Your moment so bright.
if I tell you
will you listen?
bask as I do!
I am going to follow this light
it leads us to something precious
dance as I do!
take off anything binding
your feet in the sand,
go!
all the while I am loving you.

Where my thoughts are

down I go
and still you are there
every freckle, a masterpiece
small and so great
laughing all the way down to where you wait-
does sanity allow such arrangements?
knowing what may follow each gesture
smoke and liquor fill my starlit nights
and you, golden haired and oblivious.
I am the consort of your will.
youth could have
age does have
and here I am looking at the stars,
I know I would have.

untitled 10 / 03

each moment
each breath
each glance
you move ruby lips and my soul shakes
satisfaction that is only God given
do you know it? is it possible for you
to gauge when it is inherently yours?
hearts can never prepare for such catharsis
we know we cannot repress what we did not ask for
gently moving in a direction that will turn you around
and halt your better intentions
how much can a man do before his heart
turns him back
bliss will charge an account that has
no choice but to say "that is appropriate"
it is for you
each moment
each breath
each glance.

Hmm...Buzz away

it worked
you followed like bees to honey
while all the time I was pretending you were not there
swarming, fertilizing, sweetening
stung by your presence
like nectar
so ripe to taste when finally I gave in
from nest to hive and burrow we flee
now I am following you
yes, I am.
whose honey drew you in first?
when smoke cannot chase away
And beekeepers tame their prey
the sting of love will linger
what initially brought you
will once again have its say.

fresh 12-13-05

the new arrangement finds me
strolling in the park
I see remnants of leaves
summer gives fighting demands but fall refuses to flinch even in December.
Walking in the dark , I am alone
I see lovers doing their thing
All I am thinking about is making love to you.
My mind is hearing bass and strings much too far for you to hear.
but you walk to the rhythm of my heart.
and like a dream, I only think of holding your hands by candlelight
allowing so much to pass
with my magic assistance, my desire for you has subsided.
The moon is now shining but the park is too cloudy to see.
Sullen trees drop bloody leaves on my shoulders (and yes I have bled too)
I bleed like the fruit of this strange poplar tree.
the scent of magnolia in winter is an offering I must take on this path.
for the sun to rise, I must drink again your love's wine and taste your hypnotic fruits.
for I have eaten of them and now cannot stop seeing your face.
you kept thinking you were the only one
and this makes me laugh.

connection fulfilling its duty

summer filled my day with song.
I sang a new song, and with you, the harmony was beautiful and easy.
my heart knew love.
The nights were yours and your music was full and rising and kept me moving.
Orange and sweetness filled the air.
you sang to stars that danced for you.
we kiss under a moonlit night.
you painted love onto my skin each night in new dwellings.
It was a night of firsts.
love was filling you.
The sun gave us sand and fresh fruit and escapes
from the mundane city building that you still visit.
Each magical night was a new secret space .
sacred and magical, each night was ours.
we were falling in love.
our dance in the street and our song in perfect harmony.
Each hour was to be soaked in, bathed in. But not to cleanse ourselves, rather, immerse ourselves
so that our nights, our stars, our songs, our kisses
could somehow become part of the existence
never modulate, become frivolous, lose tone or be forgotten.
and we rue the day our love was lost.
love has settled on shores that beat cold against sand
yet they warm for the arrival of the heart of new life, new songs, more shooting stars,
moonlit drives ,and harmony of souls
that find each other in summer then love through all seasons.
love is alive.

miracle

I try to act as if your absence does not greatly affect me
it seems to have passed without notice
and with great speed.
It has shaped me , yet I never had the chance to soak up what I
needed.
I am miles from there and
most of you are dead.
(some of you literally)
I want to grasp tightly that magic in your miraculous refrain-
it beats in my head
it beats in my heart;
the miracle of that time
bubbles over into now
and I cry for the original
and cope with the substitutes.

the story

It has not changed.
not for you
nor for me.
Not for those who came before us
nor for those who will follow.
We profess in different light, shades of skin, and different tongues.
The more it is told the more similar it becomes.
The variations are lost through repetition.
It is more splendid and precious and triumphant and tragic all in the same.
My interpretation is a seemingly unique story.
yet in the very loneliness it sits in, lies a unbreakable connection
to all that has been heard and told
all that will be spoken and listened to
and will be repeated in every story told
as it always has been.

glowing moon

Now the moon looks at me as if I should know what it is thinking
for many nights of many years
it has lent to me all of its secrets.
Now it is furtive and mysterious.
four points of light stream out from an icy center giving
no clues as to what may happen next.
The procession of fellows driven by strange desire have
made my eyes dull.
I have used this cold beacon to
make heat in darkened rooms with empty hearts.
Now I only have a moon that looks at me as if
I should know what it is thinking.

on my island of hopes

let me surround you
let me be the calm you see
too much I can't say
I fall from god
come here without you.
I need you so.
These words I hear are my medicine.
and you just walk away
the nights too long
cold without you with no words to say
I need you so.

right now (for DLB)

Right now I can smell you
Oh and if I suck my teeth, I taste you.
I can see your closely set pale eyes
I can see your gold hair
I feel your lips right now
Right now you permeate my thoughts.
When does not matter.
Right now you are.
Right now we are in Paris,
neither of us have been (now only I have not)
Your apprehension is not here right now
but your sweet nasal whine is.
your laugh that's nervous and sure.
you body, every piece, is here.
right now.
and right now I will sleep with you
because you are here.
right now

knowledge

making you you know
having you see
but not able to say exactly what I need.
I know with my eyes
I know with my heart
I want to return to the very start.
If I could rewind , would that even matter?
The wash of tears that just will not come, may help me
and the damage that has been done.
But you and your smile and all of the faux bliss
may never know what I felt when I felt like this.
I do not find your heart (for all that is worth)
has a piece of traceable compassion anywhere on this earth.
I thought for a moment that I was alright
But I find myself again seeing through the game and of course the lie.
You want to be wanted by all who surround
and then to have the power to leave and to drop
But like the wise have told and always say
everything you do will come back to you one day.

A brief description

Bound to this wave
it carries me once again
over and under
I submerge in your wonderful spell
night after night
finding a new star for us
please see if I am still breathing for
I am no longer certain that I am alive
Illuminated with anticipation
of another kiss.
No company to hold my interest; for there is
pattern leading us to have each other again and again.
The ending of this story becoming more and more grand
Days, sunlight, crisp wind carrying a heart's wish
from coast to coast landing in my hands like
a ladybug, tickling my skin, filling me up.
Sleep now with songs that can only be dreamt
precious, glowing, removing.

I love you

triple the amount and you will begin to know how much
It goes continuously, reaching outward.
wrapping you in cool blue.
you perceive it and shy away
yet it goes nowhere.
you call on it and get no answer
now it is all you want.
you call upon it and beckon dramatically
you write for it
Is it here or there?
anxious knees in your chest
Naked , you will sleep, but not alone
with you, thoughts will come, satisfying you completely
every need met
unwinding complexities with ease
lightly stroking your face like the wind
simply saying I love you.

My special angel

thanks to deity , for not a wish that has ever been true
could equal what stands before me now.
It could not be more special.
this muse of modern and sizeable living.
I wonder which star hanging in orange southern skies in summer
did I call upon?
Which star heard my humble cry to bring me an angel of golden brilliance?
What prayer was heeded to and what exactly did I ask for?
I knew not of such characteristics as I am merely human
while these qualities are god-like.
woven like a perfect quilt on the coldest day
you wrap me up and I know safety
next to you.

more love?

is that what you want?
is that what I have had?
empty drinks say so
empty drinks say no
filled up and emptied promptly
 faint memories so blurred by times trick
tick, tick, tick
and still I say I have never been so unsure of anything.

my sweet dreamer

are you sleeping?
that precious mouth closed
warm air escapes your nose
I want to lay down next to you
whisper in your ear
dream now
dream sweet
feel the warmth under the sun
fly above the clouds
look down to me
come down to me
kiss me
away you go as
I kiss your eyes goodnight

all of it

to remember the way it tasted
or perhaps how it felt to my lips.
to know what was in your mind
when your body tilted into me
to be brave enough to be at the beginning
and strong enough to face an end.
to look into eyes that pull me out of
my own world in hopes that this new one
will sustain me in the way
your touch does.
golden skin that beams like an angel with
a halo of matching hair.
eyes that take green and push it into your memory
smile that shows love and innocence
and also knows pain and rejection and humility.
hands to feel my back against you nightly
or was it all a dream?
sweetness and dusk dampen my heart that beats irregularly these
days;
too fast and at times with such a pace that it may as well not beat at
all.
every angle is studied
it's perfection should be repeated to any who know me.
All I have ever experienced stops meaning half as much.
Enchanted one that holds my gaze and makes of it what it wishes.
will left hold right?

About The Author

To say that my life is a work process would be accurate. I have always done some form of creative expression, art or interpretaion that lends itself to different forms of thought. All the while keeping a sense of folly at heart." When I was scouting musical acts in my early twenties I thought that would be all I was going to do in life. Quickly my interests changed and my work had to reflect that change. I had no inclination in regards to my following jobs and work, at least on a conscious level. From being an actor to writing poetry, I just sort of follow what feels most appropriate and is most harmonious with the integrity of who I am.

I loved writing this material simply because it reflected all that was taking place in my life at those moments. Even the most painful of experiences were lightened in the rearranging of the thought to free form poetry. Falling in love is an experience everyone has felt and knows there exists an inexplicable series of emotion, thought and temptations that I have tried to embody with words. Essentially what I have done is taken what was to be a literal flat journal entry and interpreted them as abstract pieces in the hopes that I might gain a new perspective of my own emotional process of being lovestruck, elated, heartbroken and renewed.

*Corey won a SAG Award for his acting in the Academy Award winning "Traffic" and was the lead of the acclaimed indie flick "Journey Of Jared Price."

*He is currently studying psychology in Los Angeles and continues to seek out more artistic endeavors.

Colophon

Text: Minion Pro
Titles: Warehouse
Set in Adobe Indesign
Printed in USA

www.onespiritpress.com
onespiritpress@gmail.com

www.ingramcontent.com/pod-product-compliance
Lightning Source LLC
Chambersburg PA
CBHW062009070426
42451CB00008BA/336